MG 4.5 0.5pt.

INSIDE MLB

CHICAGO CUBS

K. C. Kelley

MEDIA ENHANCED BOOKS

AV2 BY WEIGL™

ADDED VALUE • AUDIO VISUAL

www.av2books.com

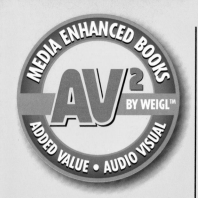

AV² provides enriched content that supplements and complements this book. Weigl's AV² books strive to create inspired learning and engage young minds in a total learning experience.

Your AV² Media Enhanced books come alive with...

Audio
Listen to sections of the book read aloud.

Key Words
Study vocabulary, and complete a matching word activity.

Go to **www.av2books.com**, and enter this book's unique code.

Video
Watch informative video clips.

Quizzes
Test your knowledge.

BOOK CODE

N 8 3 7 3 9 2

Embedded Weblinks
Gain additional information for research.

Slide Show
View images and captions, and prepare a presentation.

AV² by Weigl brings you media enhanced books that support active learning.

Try This!
Complete activities and hands-on experiments.

... and much, much more!

Published by AV² by Weigl
350 5th Avenue, 59th Floor
New York, NY 10118
Website: www.av2books.com

Library of Congress Cataloging-in-Publication Data

Names: Kelley, K. C., author. | Willis, John, author.
Title: Chicago Cubs / K.C. Kelley, John Willis.
Description: New York, NY : AV2 by Weigl, [2017] | Series: Inside MLB | Includes index.
Identifiers: LCCN 2016051913 (print) | LCCN 2017002500 (ebook) | ISBN 9781489659385 (hard cover : alk. paper) | ISBN 9781489659392 (soft cover : alk. paper) | ISBN 9781489659408 (multi-user ebk.)
Subjects: LCSH: Chicago Cubs (Baseball team)--History--Juvenile literature.
Classification: LCC GV875.C6 K453 2017 (print) | LCC GV875.C6 (ebook) | DDC 796.357/640977311--dc23
LC record available at https://lccn.loc.gov/2016051913

Printed in the United States of America in Brainerd, Minnesota
1 2 3 4 5 6 7 8 9 0   21 20 19 18 17

022017
020117

Project Coordinator: John Willis   Designer: Nick Newton

Contents

GO, CUBS!

The Cubs have been in Chicago for more than 100 years. They won the **World Series** in 2016. This was the first time they had won a World Series since 1908! Their fans continue to be **loyal** and loud. The "Cubbies" are among baseball's best-loved teams. Let's meet the Cubs!

It took a full seven games for the Cubs to win the 2016 World Series. The last game lasted for 10 innings and included a rain delay.

In 1922, the **Chicago Cubs** beat the **Philadelphia Phillies** **26–23** in the highest-scoring game in **MLB history**.

Third baseman Kris Bryant was drafted by the Chicago Cubs in 2013. He was part of the team that won the 2016 World Series.

Who Are the Cubs?

The Chicago Cubs are a team in baseball's National League (NL). The NL joins with the American League (AL) to form Major League Baseball. The Cubs play in the Central Division of the NL. The division winners and two wild-card teams get to play in the league playoffs. The playoff winners from the two leagues face off in the World Series. The Cubs have won three World Series championships.

The **Chicago Cubs** won **6** of the first **11** **NL Championships**.

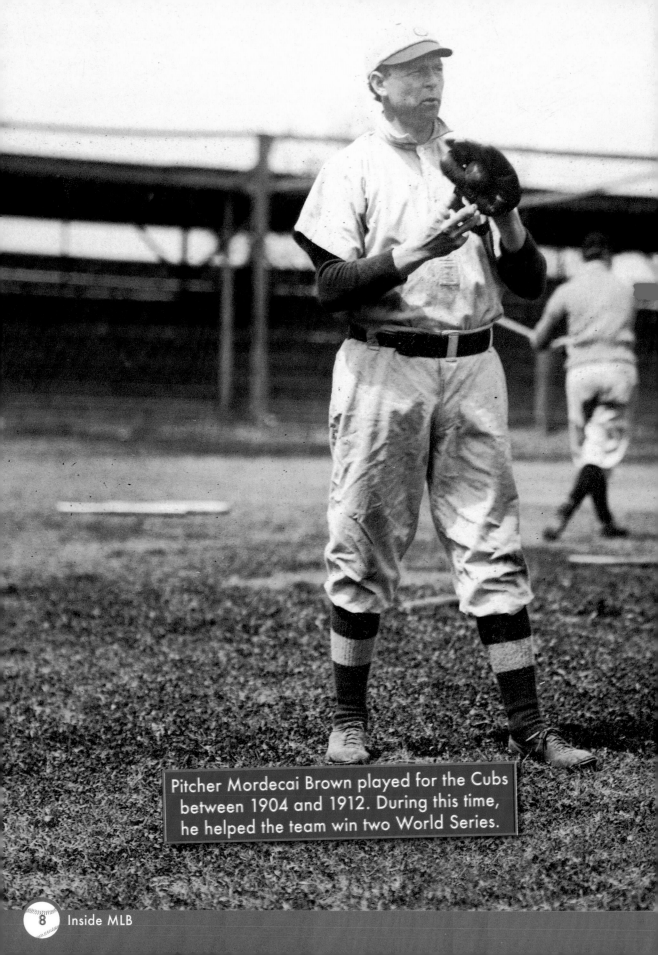

Pitcher Mordecai Brown played for the Cubs between 1904 and 1912. During this time, he helped the team win two World Series.

WHERE THEY CAME FROM

The Chicago Cubs haven't always been the Cubs. The NL had its first season in 1876. The Chicago White Stockings played in that first NL season. They became the Colts in 1890, then the Orphans in 1898. Finally, in 1903, they got their current name. The Cubs have always played in Chicago. They have been in their current ballpark longer than any other NL team.

In 2016, the Chicago Cubs ended the season with a record of 103–58. They also had one tied game, against the Pittsburgh Pirates.

Who They Play

The Chicago Cubs play 162 games each season. That includes about 19 games against each of the other teams in their division. The Cubs have won four NL Central championships. The other NL Central teams are the Cincinnati Reds, the Milwaukee Brewers, the Pittsburgh Pirates, and the St. Louis Cardinals. The Cubs and the Cardinals are big **rivals**. Their games always get the fans charged up! The Cubs also play some teams from the AL. Their AL **opponents** change every year.

The first **post-season** game between the **Cubs** and the **Cardinals** was held in **2015**.

Where They Play

Wrigley Field has been the home of the Cubs since 1914. It is the oldest ballpark in the NL. Many of the walls are made of brick. The **outfield** fence is covered with bright green ivy plants! Some buildings are very close to Wrigley Field. Fans can sit on their roofs to watch the game! The area around the beloved ballpark is fun on game days. It's called "Wrigleyville." The ballpark was the last in the majors to get lights for night baseball. Until 1988, all Cubs home games were day games!

The **scoreboard** at **Wrigley Field** has **never** been hit by a **batted ball**.

Wrigley Field's scoreboard was built in 1937 and is still in use today. The numbers on the board are changed by hand.

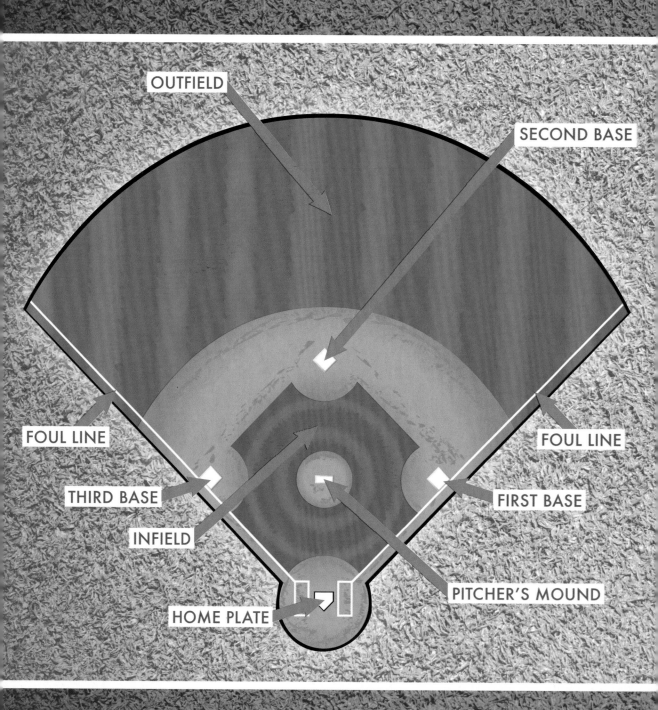

OUTFIELD

SECOND BASE

FOUL LINE

FOUL LINE

THIRD BASE

FIRST BASE

INFIELD

PITCHER'S MOUND

HOME PLATE

THE BASEBALL DIAMOND

Baseball games are played on a field called a diamond. Four bases form this diamond shape. The bases are 90 feet (27 meters) apart. The area around and between the bases is called the infield. At the center of the infield is the pitcher's mound. The grass area beyond the bases is called the outfield. White lines start at **home plate** and go toward the outfield. These are the foul lines. Baseballs hit outside these lines are out of play unless a fielder catches them. The outfield walls are about 300–450 feet (91–137 m) from home plate.

Big Days

The Cubs have had some good seasons in their history. Here are three of them:

1907: *A Cubs team led by great pitching won back-to-back World Series championships.*

2007: *The Cubs made the playoffs two seasons in a row. It was the first time they had done that in 100 years. However, they lost all their games in those two playoff series.*

2016: *The Chicago Cubs' 2016 season was one for the history books. They won 103 of their regular-season games. This success landed them in the World Series. The series was hard-won, with the Cubs trailing the Cleveland Indians three games to one. Yet, the Cubs rallied to win the final three games. This ended their 108-year World Series drought.*

The Cubs' 2016 World Series win ended the longest title drought in North American professional sports history.

In 1945, the Chicago Cubs ended the regular season with a 98-56 record. They won the NL pennant, but failed to capture the World Series title.

Tough Days

The Cubs have had a lot of tough seasons. Here are three of the worst:

1962: *The Cubs lost 103 games, their worst record ever. They finished next to last in the NL.*

2003: *The Cubs were leading 3–0 in the eighth inning. A win would take them to the World Series. But a fan tried to grab a foul ball that would have ended the inning. The Florida Marlins won the game. The Cubs would go on to lose the entire series to the Marlins the following night.*

2013: *In 2013, the Cubs suffered their lowest attendance numbers in 10 years. Fans were growing tired of the losses. They lost 96 games and finished in fifth place for the fourth year in a row.*

MEET THE FANS

Cubs fans are among some of the most loyal in baseball. They had to be. Their team had not won a title in 108 years. They pack Wrigley Field for Cubs games. They started a baseball tradition more than 50 years ago. When an opponent hits a home run into the stands, the fans throw it back!

Fans at Cubs games can often be heard singing "Go, Cubs, Go," written by Steve Goodman. It has become the unofficial Cubs victory song.

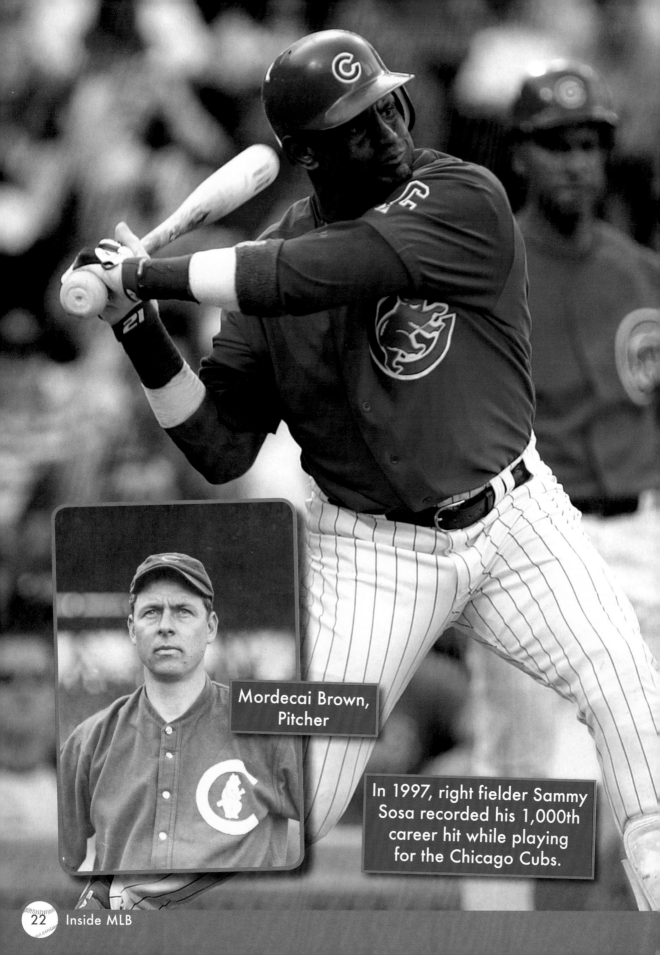

Mordecai Brown, Pitcher

In 1997, right fielder Sammy Sosa recorded his 1,000th career hit while playing for the Chicago Cubs.

Heroes Then...

In the 1880s and 1890s, Chicago's Cap Anson was one of the best all-around players. He was the first player to reach 3,000 hits in a career. Mordecai Brown was called "Three-Finger" because he had hurt his hand in a farming accident. He pitched for the Cubs from 1904 to 1912. In 1930, Hack Wilson had 191 runs batted in (RBI). That's still the most ever in one season. In the 1950s and 1960s, Ernie Banks earned the nickname "Mr. Cub." A slugging infielder, he was loved by the fans. One of his favorite sayings was, "It's a beautiful day for a ballgame . . . Let's play two!" In the 1980s, second baseman Ryne Sandberg was a **Gold Glove** fielder, a top base stealer, and a home run slugger. In the late 1990s and early 2000s, Sammy Sosa had three seasons with 60 or more homers.

Heroes Now...

The Cubs' roster is made up of solid players. Pitcher Jake Arrieta continues to lead the Cubs to victories. He was awarded the **Cy Young Award** in 2015 and pitched 190 strikeouts in the 2016 season. First baseman Anthony Rizzo is another star of the Chicago Cubs. Rizzo is a three-time MLB **All-Star.** In 2015, he recorded 72 extra-base hits, the most for a Cubs left-handed hitter since 1972. Third baseman Kris Bryant was drafted by the Chicago Cubs in the first round of the 2013 draft. He made his MLB debut in 2015. That year, he received the **Rookie of the Year** award. He set franchise rookie records with 26 home runs, 99 RBIs, and 273 total bases. Veteran Ben Zobrist was named the World Series Most Valuable Player (MVP) in 2016 for his stellar performance in the series.

The present-day Cubs are loaded with star players.

Kris Bryant, Third Base

Anthony Rizzo, First Baseman

Jake Arrieta, Pitcher

GEARING UP

Baseball players all wear a team jersey and pants. They have to wear a team hat in the field and a helmet when batting. Take a look at Ben Zobrist and Willson Contreras to see some other parts of a baseball player's uniform.

CATCHER'S MASK

CATCHER'S CHEST PROTECTOR

CATCHER'S MITT

CATCHER'S SHIN GUARD

Willson Contreras, Catcher

BAT

BATTING HELMET

BATTING GLOVES

TEAM JERSEY

TEAM PANTS

Ben Zobrist,
Second Base

BASEBALL CLEATS

SPORTS STATS

Here are some all-time career records for the Chicago Cubs. All of the stats are through the 2016 season.

A Major League baseball weighs about **5 ounces** (142 grams). It is **9 inches** (23 centimeters) around. A leather cover surrounds **hundreds** of feet of string. That string is wound around a small center of **rubber** and **cork**.

Home Runs

Sammy Sosa, **545**

Ernie Banks, **512**

Runs Batted In

Cap Anson, **1,880**

Ernie Banks, **1,636**

Batting Average
Bill Madlock, **.336**
Riggs Stephenson, **.336**

Stolen Bases
Frank Chance, **402**
Bill Lange, **400**

Wins by a Pitcher
Charlie Root, **201**
Mordecai Brown, **188**

Wins by a Manager
Cap Anson, **1,282**

Earned Run Average
Mordecai Brown, **1.80**
Jack Pfiester, **1.85**

Quiz

1 How long did the Cubs go without a championship win?

2 In which year did the Cubs break their championship drought?

3 The Cubs are part of which league?

4 Where do the Cubs play?

5 Which Cubs player had the nickname of "Three-Finger"?

6 How many home runs did Sammy Sosa make in his career with the Cubs?

7 Who leads the Cubs in stolen bases?

8 Who holds the Cubs record for the most wins by a pitcher?

Answers

1. 108 years
2. 2016
3. The National League
4. Wrigley Field
5. Mordecai Brown
6. 545
7. Frank Chance
8. Charlie Root

Key Words

All-Star: a player who is selected to play in a yearly game between the best players in each league

Cy Young Award: award given to the top pitcher in each league

Gold Glove: an award given to the top fielder at each position in each league

home plate: a five-sided rubber pad where batters stand to swing

loyal: supporting something no matter what

opponents: the teams or players that play against each other

outfield: the large grassy area beyond the infield of a baseball diamond

rivals: teams that play each other often and have an ongoing competition

Rookie of the Year: an award given to the top first-year player in each league

World Series: the Major League Baseball championship

Index

Log on to www.av2books.com

AV² by Weigl brings you media enhanced books that support active learning. Go to www.av2books.com, and enter the special code found on page 2 of this book. You will gain access to enriched and enhanced content that supplements and complements this book. Content includes video, audio, weblinks, quizzes, a slide show, and activities.

AV² Online Navigation

Book Pages
AV² pages directly correspond to pages in the book.

Audio
Listen to sections of the book read aloud.

Video
Watch informative video clips.

Embedded Weblinks
Gain additional information for research.

Key Words
Study vocabulary, and complete a matching word activity.

Quizzes
Test your knowledge.

Slide Show
View images and captions, and prepare a presentation.

Try This!
Complete activities and hands-on experiments.

AV² was built to bridge the gap between print and digital. We encourage you to tell us what you like and what you want to see in the future.

Sign up to be an AV² Ambassador at www.av2books.com/ambassador.

Due to the dynamic nature of the Internet, some of the URLs and activities provided as part of AV² by Weigl may have changed or ceased to exist. AV² by Weigl accepts no responsibility for any such changes. All media enhanced books are regularly monitored to update addresses and sites in a timely manner. Contact AV² by Weigl at 1-866-649-3445 or av2books@weigl.com with any questions, comments, or feedback.